ITALY

Text and photographs by
Chris Fairclough

General Editor
Henry Pluckrose

Franklin Watts
London   New York   Sydney   Toronto

Words about Italy

Alps
anchovies
Apennine
  mountains
autostrade

Bologna
Bolognese sauce

canneloni
Chianti
Colosseum

Dolomites

Fiat
Florence

gelato
gondolas

Gorgonzola
Grand Canal

La Scala
lira

Mediterranean
  Sea
Michelangelo
Milan
Mount Vesuvius

Naples

olive oil

Parmesan cheese
pasta
Pisa
Pompeii

Pope

ravioli
River Po
Riviera
Roman Catholic
Rome (Roma)

St Peter's
  Cathedral
sardines
Sardinia
spaghetti
Sicily

tuna
Turin

Vatican City
Venice

Franklin Watts Limited
8 Cork Street
London W1

ISBN UK edition: 0 85166 920 4
ISBN US edition: 0 531 04319 3
Library of Congress Catalog Card No:
81–50031

© Franklin Watts Limited 1981

Printed in Great Britain by
E. T. Heron, Essex and London

Maps by Brian and Constance Dear, and
Tony Payne.
Design by Tim Healey.
The author and publisher would like to
thank the following for kind permission to
reproduce photographs: Italian State
Tourist Board (20, 29, 30); C.I.T.
(England) Ltd (cover, 3, 5, 14, 15, 18, 28,
31); Fiat (23); Ian Goodwin (25); Graeme
Redrup (22).
The author would also like to thank
Maralisa Sassi.

Italy is a long peninsula (finger of
land) jutting into the Mediterranean
Sea. It includes two large islands
offshore: Sicily and Sardinia. Italy
is in southern Europe, so the climate
is generally warm.

Rome is the capital of Italy, and also its largest city. Its Italian name is Roma. Nearly 3 million people live and work here, and the streets are full of traffic. In summer the city is thronged with tourists.

Rome was once the heart of the ancient Roman Empire. The city has many historic buildings. This is the Colosseum. It was built by the Romans as a sports stadium.

Vatican City is a tiny state in Rome. The Pope lives and works here. He is the head of the Roman Catholic Church. People come from all over the world to visit and pray in St Peter's Cathedral.

Most Italians are Roman Catholics. Churches are beautifully decorated with rich gilt and polished marble. St Peter's Cathedral is shown above.

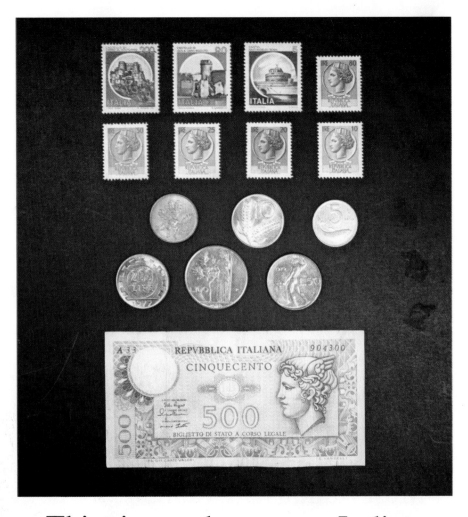

This picture shows some Italian
stamps and money. The main unit
of money is the lira. A single lira will
buy very little.

WORLD MAP

Italy

FRANCE SWITZERLAND AUSTRIA

ALPS

Milan

Dolomites

Venice

YUGOSLAVIA

Turin

River Po

Bologna

Pisa Florence

ITALY

ADRIATIC SEA

Rome
Roma

APENNINES

Naples

Pompeii

SARDINIA

MEDITERRANEAN SEA

SICILY

9

Italian children start primary school when they are six. Most schools are run by the state. Many private schools are run by the Roman Catholic Church.

Italian families are often very
large. Grandparents and other
relations may live in the same house.
At meal times, the whole family sits
down together around the same
table.

Most families eat some kind of
pasta every day. Pasta is made from
flour, water, eggs and oil. It can be
home-made, but today most Italians
buy it from shops.

12

Spaghetti is the best known type of pasta. Others include ravioli and canneloni. Sauces poured over pasta are called after the place they first came from. For example, Bolognese sauce is from Bologna.

Italy has a long coastline with many fishing villages, so fish dishes are eaten in many parts of the country. Cheeses are popular too. Creamy Gorgonzola and Parmesan are two of the best known.

Italy's warm hillsides are ideal for growing vines. The grapes are harvested to make wine. A famous wine called Chianti is sold in round-bottomed bottles that are covered with straw.

The Italians love ice cream. It is sold everywhere in many varieties: vanilla, fruits, chocolate, nuts and berries – sometimes all mixed together. Ice cream is called "gelato" in Italian.

The Italians are keen sports fans. Football and motor racing draw huge crowds. Italian boys play football everywhere, even in the streets.

Many Italian towns were built long ago and their narrow streets were not made for modern traffic. Shopkeepers often display their goods in the open. This one is a shop selling copper pots and pans.

18

Motor scooters are a popular way of getting about in Italian towns. They are noisy, but cheap to run. They are also easy to weave through traffic in narrow or crowded streets.

There are many fine beaches on Italy's long coastline. The northwest coast around Genoa is called the Italian Riviera. It is always crowded with holidaymakers in summer from Italy and abroad.

Inland, much of Italy is hilly or mountainous. The Apennine mountains run down through the middle of Italy, and the high Alps lie to the north. Motorways are called autostrade. High bridges carry them across the valleys.

The towering Alps mark Italy's
northern border. Holidaymakers
visit them for their winter sports,
and for walking and climbing in
summer. The craggy peaks of the
Dolomites are on the eastern fringe
of the Alps.

Italy's main industrial cities are in the northwest, in the broad and fertile valley of the River Po. Turin is the heart of the Italian motor industry. Many cars are exported. Fiat is the largest car firm.

Milan, in the northwest, is a thriving trading city. It is the second largest city in Italy. The great opera house of La Scala is shown here. Italians are known for their love of opera and have created many great operas.

Florence in the northwest was famous for its artists in the 14th to 16th centuries. The city has many fine museums and galleries. The great sculptor and artist, Michelangelo, worked here. This is a picture of his "David".

The leaning tower of Pisa, near Florence, is one of the best known buildings in Italy. Over the years it has slowly sunk on one side. However, visitors may still walk up the steps to the top.

Venice is built on many islands around the Grand Canal. There are no roads, so people get about by boat. Gondolas are slender vessels pushed along by poles.

Southern Italy is a hotter and
poorer region than the north. Most
people work on the land, raising
livestock or growing such crops as
olives, grapes and citrus fruits. Many
live in crowded hilltop villages.

Naples lies on the southwest coast. It is the third largest city in Italy, and its busy shipping industry handles Italian exports such as wine, cheese, pasta and olive oil. On the outskirts there are slums where the poor live.

Pompeii is an ancient city near Naples. In AD 79 it was buried in ash from a volcanic eruption at nearby Mount Vesuvius. Now, the ash has been cleared. The city is an open air museum.

Sicily is a large island off the southern tip of Italy. Fishing is an important industry. Sicily produces tuna, sardines and anchovies. Here, a fisherman mends his nets beside the sea wall. The fishing boats used are usually small.

Index